DISCIPLINE

DISCIPLINE

DAWN LUNDY MARTIN

WINNER OF THE 2009 NIGHTBOAT POETRY PRIZE

NIGHTBOAT BOOKS

CALLICOON, NEW YORK

Foreword

In his introduction to *Bottom Dogs* by Edward Dahlberg, D.H. Lawrence writes: "What the young feel intensely, and no longer so secretly, is the extreme repulsiveness of other people." He wrote this in 1929 in the wake of the Great Depression and ascribed this condition to an erosion of mutual sympathy among American citizens after decades of exploitation and violence directed towards the earth and others.

This many years later, his words evoke our nation now. How can artists respond to the loathing that trickles down to the youngest of the young? In the case of *Discipline*, the poet responds directly and personally, discovering the larger trauma in the materials of her own life. She is heroic because of her refusal to hide or escape from a single, fatal moment. Like Antigone. This is her mission. It is a modern story, composed in the frenzy of potential suicide and agitated despair. She makes her path straight by her continual running back and forth, carrying her outrage.

You can remember, reading this book, the nausea once identified by Sartre and certainly by Dahlberg. This nausea has lain dormant since students took to the streets in 1968. But it has not been nowhere. It is firmly planted in the racialized American experience, in segregation and the continued interference with the bodies and progress of girls and women.

This book digs into the roots of our culture by entering its pivotal derangement, just as Antigone enters the cave/grave, and I don't see how it could dig further. Down there it is hard to see, and one feels one's way blindly and only by touch, a touch jerking with repulsion and guided only by memory, not prophecy. A courageous act of feeling is what we have here, and a return of the rejected person as a recognizable companion.

Fanny Howe

excreta

[or sentence] or ripe:

here the mouth held

grip over

and flood liquid

a defecated magic

(everything said was surprising)

cosmologica in seconds

in breath-attempts under weight metal

here the jar

here the inside of the jar

excruciation fixed

[or phrase] or doubt:

three went in and three emerged although significantly reduced

dispossession fragrance like mules or dung

When one is told the structure or the method and the staggering
absence of, or the omnipresent existence of, it becomes difficult
to get on the subway or bathe one's own body. These are acts of
forgetting, though they appear to be acts of resistance or love.

0110000101110101011101000110111 0

1100010011010010110111101100111 01

1100100110000101110000011010000110

1001011001010111001100100000011011

1101100110001000000110000100 10000

0011000100110111101100100011111001

Not so much a name, but the result of a name. As a metaphor for the eyes' inward, turning. It might say what the thing is, or it might not know. So then. Heritage as fantasy. That the seer looks toward a past—markers of it—in food and location, in wrecked bodies, flesh strung, etc. A want toward warmth. Highways of sun through windows. Where it might not reach. So when I imagine the father as a boy—he said, in fields, a child. And here the hand holds an infant (his?) and jumps from a very tall building, or threatens to jump, in the name of something believed.

Bodies in uncommon strobes. What mystery in jaunty bodies. (Or are they murderous bodies? Who can tell? I can't tell.) Streaming video. Private locations. Large hard hands inserted in zippers. There's unrecognizable scent. There were are. A. We. There. A timeless we. A we of all. On a wall. We that drift in and out of doors and into musty bathrooms that feel wet all the time. How many ordinances exist? Local communities flailing. Screaming into night as would fish into night.

What kind of brilliant stare in their scrubbed features, their lips smacking on creamed cheeses? I want to laugh but repulsion invades the body and makes it want to pee. Every silent wailing could find its place in these acts. Where the other meats the self. Meat-flesh. *Just order the fucking latte.* I am a living example— bootstrap fool, hanger-on-er. (Is there a thing to recover?)

National dialogues on the blotting screen, everywhere's down from here, they say, unless, unless. A voice is bare, inaudible. It mouths, *my father is half his normal weight and in a bed in Hartford Hospital.* Hollows or glass. Fragments of being. Being or nothing. Near not being. Precisely what the body resists the body is. They turn the television on for comfort. They tuck the sheets and pull them into neat corners, its edges of order. We had a house full of books.

A sick man vomits into a cup at McDonald's in Union Square and it's hard to feel sorry for him because he's so public. Once, when I was a teenager, a friend pointed to a doddering black man on the street and said laughing, What if that guy was your father? It was.

Mothers warn against usual dangers. Men and the sun. Rough hands of the friend shield against strangers. It becomes difficult to imagine a harmful stranger. You are supposed to write an essay titled "Dirty Love" but you can't because you are exhausted by him—the friend—his attic apartment, his slack bathrobe, his rum and cokes, and Kent cigarettes. Your skin was lighter when you were eleven and you were more desirable. Fluorescent supermarket lights make the whole thing worse. Reflection's comeuppance.

Before the effort in desire, one hurries into the porn store and then hurries out again. She is the only one hurrying. Everyone else is motionless. (Recover-y) (ing) One remembers being someone's girl. The possession of someone else. That kind of safety. For what? Then? Flapfplap of pages turning. Here is the size of a hole. Here is the size of what happened before. And of no one watching.

Everyday it happens or doesn't happen. The I struggles to become a part of the reeking body. The body drifts off to fuck like a ghost. In countries with barriers, an attack, unwarranted. Wrists held tight behind the back. Great views from the wooden window toward whatever.

Iowa,

strict Jesus

a cock stinking belligerently.

In December, lights blanket snowing streets. A dark girl under cover of white. There is no world outside of this. Walls of white and white bliss, flakes sting skin, undeniable and wanted. We could find incidents toward exigencies. Moments that should urge, compel. Which accumulated evidences would suffice? There are bodies stuffed in trees—we know that. We see them when we do not anticipate them. Hungry and echoing into chilled air.

We pass cities in the middles of nowheres. We know them by their smokestacks, wires, and infernos burning atop holes in the sky. White families post Private and No Trespassing signs in their front yards. I want to yell out the window, *I am both very alive and very dead! I am a suspect! Why has no one named me as a suspect!* There is a disappearance so incrementally slow no one notices. A left hand touching the right hand, a touching and being touched, a consideration of which.

So tell me, it sings, *how can I live forever?* When a man is trapped as words are trapped in the defect of the body, when hundreds of untold stories make the body convex, ape out, indulge in excess so that the mouth is never empty, when the grass of youth is so far away, a tale of a tale of a tale, when thinning out drags the skin, when a life, a life so small it is disremembered, scant and numbered, framed by ritual, the steps to the cellar refrigerator, the heaves of breath, and the particular and unordinary love for a daughter more than a reach away, when derelict is as wasting away, when sleeves of abandon mask the face, when one speaks into drapes and wind, whispers against drift, unheard, when almost everything, every small and huge thing is in one room, one insubstantial place covered by a roof that leaks through a gunhole when thunderous rain, when it is this life and there is the infrequent kiss of the absent daughter, and there is the singular desire of not forever, maybe, but just one more minute after minute, when there is simply, is.

What we didn't know then is the quality of sound when it was silence and that disturbs us now, especially me, the silence of what might have occurred if it were—or if—fuck, I don't know, something different, or something spoken that wasn't. What can I say now, even, of blame? Every concrete image has to do with a house or a door or a hallway. What we didn't know is that there are cars with opaque windows, that one can crawl into a big old American Buick and not be seen. I can say, perhaps, that there was a woman, and it is you, that you rode the long way from a southern state and never smoked or drank whiskey. What we didn't know is that there is a kind of silence in obedience. Pages get raveled and unraveled, so even the written and disposed of, is again. On a street, there are other dumb lucks, the boy who we tied to a tree and whipped with a rope, as a game, and there he was flailing from the sting of it, in shorts, and saying, no, no. What we didn't know then, is that a mother, you, maybe, or some other mother, looked up into a blue, cloudless sky, and remembered a snake under a pail and small terrors.

0110100001100101011100100110010101/011

0001101101111011011100111010001011001

01011011010111000001101111011100100

1100001011100100111001/01100010011

0110001101001011001110110100001101

00 0 0110001001101111011110011011100011

Woolen cloth. Unworkable. Hard and scratchy. Doesn't act like much. Not a rug or a blanket. The smell of mold. Covering on walls, the walls, grey and raised, a pattern one can never forget. Fingertips can never forget. A kind of wall that might become you. You might become it—non-intricate weave, a sullen protest, against what, is unknown.

Is there or not, in the industrial fire flaming night, a dark hooded boy?

Like X equals one or seven equals Y, the kind of thing you never knew you didn't know until it presents itself. That's the way ignorance works, right? The life that happens and ordinary knowing and then there's a confrontation with the opaque— motionless square that surrounds, encloses, and prevents any seeing outside.

Illness is measured in ability, how much the body can do. Can you still go to work? Are you productive? Do you stay in bed every day or just some days? All day or part of the day? Day or night? What do you do there? Whose eye did you poke out? Which lids were broken? What color are your stockings? How many times do you wear them before you wash them? Indicate the hands on the clock ticking. Indicate which things are broken and which are already fixed. How many black waves riddle the body each day? What is your definition of a common cold? Who's out there and who's in here? Are you sure? You have to be sure.

Dollop of doll that hung, had hung—without certainty—as things hang anyway. Said "dissilient," "sheared," for cuts and other present wounds. Utterance as a hive, a bundled thought. Bro, they called him, brother, for blood and a place to land when the weather got hot, or hated, or he was hated, brrrrrrrr, bro, bruised brother, and the dolls that are headless for him. He opens his mouth as would a hewn structure, a crack in a thing so swollen it betrays the soul, becomes all body, brutal body, brutal sideway.

He opens his mouth to sing a non-threatening song, something overheard, a mother's song, but it was broken too, more of a kuff ka—kaffter kuff kuff kaffir ka, brace in the thought, the thorax.

You can take what they give you or you can fuck the whole world maybe even yourself. Just open the mouth square and press pills toward back of tongue tube the throat and imagine an easy procedure. Everything's digital now and precise. Nothing to fear. Date rape won't ruin you. The I is a condensed system. If you follow the instructions you can't accidentally overdose. Grey Goose centuries yell into speech. *You're perfect! You're fucking perfect!* Either way walking is like swimming though Delaware and you barely notice. Mine is a dagger buried in my parents' backyard. Door spills open, oil pool leagues and a tiny body wades around, listless.

How casual it all seems now, the dentists and bar bills, steel steps of a corner grocery, faces of jokers and con men, twenties arranged in a leather clip. How casual and lovely in the lure of this caustic light. Coaxing light.

If I am laden and rock hard, what will wind be? How will I know it? If I am quandary and spite and malice, among the collection of beer cans with tiny faces and an odor that clings to me, will the room become larger? All protruding logic. Inevitable gap. Burgeoning misstep. How unquestionably miserly.

What kinds of secrets, my love?

This is a partial history of fabulously forgetting. We drift inside dreams to escape the dislogic of hunger. Cracked bodies dislodge out of—well, ice cream parlors, telephone booths, husks and fabrics made for shields. Mouths made crisp from drought. A who we are not. My brother's house is hip-deep in the worry of objects. To arrive there is a past death. Is whirring uncontrollably in red night. Is being removed. Is naked canopies.

A young woman's back against a car door. A hand atop the head.
A pushing down to the knees. Trembling thighs.

Which pain?
(Stumble.)
Frequency of delivery.
The mouth opens.
It moves without agency.
Distant prattle.
A winnowing.
Brown body in white haze.
Days that feel like forgiveness.
One does not remember the face.
The body's scent is christening.
~~We will begin newly~~. (scratch that)
This is the shape of the body.
Its remembrance of its molding.
Enactment is like saying, *Yes*.

I'm trying to figure out what I have control over and what I don't, when it's possible to say, "I can't help it." I'm addicted to many things: television, alcohol, cigarettes, affection, the night.... They're not as much physical as psychological. I'm a mess. I can't help it. A narrative of melting. A narrative of Belize. A narrative of almost anything. Of sick hearts burning out of their skin. Or a brawning. Handsome boy. Brown outs are rare. I have been dreaming of the sea. The ground rises up. The methodical fashion whores are so severe. Red like meat. Magic meat. All dripping and fantastic. It's all so fantastic. Forgive me. My mind is littered with confetti. I'm concerned with the breakdown in connections between things that were once connected but no longer are. A blue fish in a blue sea. There are finite numbers of things.

People are fond of saying, Everything happens for a reason, which is complete bullshit. Required reading dots the bookshelf. There's Fanon breathing holes into us. And my brother reading in the halty sidesteps of a grade schooler. I know what my brother smells like when he's sick, angling for air, his body deep in the sweat of acquiescence. I want him to be someone else. My father liked to blame any crime in our neighborhood on "American blacks." When he mumbled under his breath, I think he was saying "Goddamned niggers," but I can't be sure.

Hindrance of the dreaded. Fortitude and enemy alliances. A free man (some say he's shackled) walks into the me in the subway station and steals something, I'm not sure what. At home, the house tangs of the dead. We never mention the way the rooms wilt with it. We paint the floor, collect the beer cans from the basement, and look sad. All five things have been distributed: a Timex watch, $152.32 in coins, a wallet photo from 1974, a certain longing, a bathrobe.

Hands,
how many?
There are hands that hold
nothing but light, and hands
that stake claims as if staking were logic.

You are in the face of something magnificent. Accept this magnificence. Lucky bastard. *Welcome to Catatonia!* The city drips its sparkling blood at the feet. Instead, one procrastinates like a goat remembering how central Florida casts its long—swings itself toward—and the scent of it, funny stripes. A mother says, "we lived in a completely segregated community and everything was regular and no one killed anyone."

The I is
more relaxed
when it is hunted.

0110010001100001011100100110101101011011
01110011001010111001101110011/01110
0000110110001100001011000110110 0101

—or, fat-choked skin

lounges against wire fence

orifice undone

a location like any other location

incidents in the midst of   unkempt propulsion

what is your ancestral stock?

I am here, too, contracted muscles

I simplify things by pretending to resist

or, *what are your measurements, then?*

try to count backward from this

try fixation on isolating the parts of the body

try glue guns and known systems

periodically, a different seismology

[great gaping things]

the I wants what it wants

hem-drag or, what errs on the side of attachment

Preening and primordial, this is our zoo. The organs in a fit of attempted resistance. Saying to each other, let me. If permission is granted, it is only temporary. An official language describes it all: multiple growths, diseased marrow, these percentages, survival, and what denotes healthy. So, comb the hair. When he returned from the hospital the first time, hair matted and down his neck, I cut my father's ridged hair in the kitchen with electric clippers. While the blood perverts, we get control of a single fluttering mass.

At the window, she bellows because it is something to do. Glittering phenomenon outside the window. Symmetry between what is outside and what is inside, that likeness or coagulation, stretches into what one could call saturation. A woman in the window is seen from the glittering ground outside the window, her mouth clearly open, sounds clearly emanating. We say broken witness. The woman enters the space once empty, occupies brown space with other brownness, both in abstraction. So, we say, if the space and the woman are brown, what happens to the empty? I, too, am often misrecognized in the dark, even here, where I had believed I was known or at least would not be mistaken. It's a strange sensation to yell out, This is me, at the very moment of being mis-seen and human but otherly so.

This is how much fortuitiveness weighs. Measure in dirt. Of vices and other habits. Of leaving a house at 3 am and drawn as would any tether and here is your lock, my dear. I want to say this plainly: it is only when I am in a woman's arms that my body is not a threat. Neither crosses nor damnation. Fix nor flutter. Hangs here, this balance, and one opens the car door and drives along the river where it said a crossing might happen. Had happened. Many times. Sticklers will say, not here. There are no crossings here. But, there the I is, reflection and delivered, on the other side. Like hams, holding on to what was.

Before the whelp

of a certain bird, the crack of morning,

the body's milking loss.

If there is prayer, there is a mother kneeling, hands folded to a private sign. We recognize it. If there is a mother kneeling, hands a tent, she is praying or she is crying or crying and praying at the same time. Although it is recognized, the signals of it, it is private and no one knows, perhaps not even she, the content of the prayer, and perhaps its object. If there is a mother praying, she is on her knees over some object, as she does not often pray in the middle of the room. One prays at the window or over the bed, the head bent slightly up or down, the eyes open or closed. This is a prayer for prayers, you know, a wanting something equal to a prayer, even though I am not a mother.

They watch a girl slip into a car and close their shades. Before. Slides. Figures insist on nothing. Impotent men live in the house. The older one beats the younger one until he surrenders as would paper. Finally, all is quiet. No more weeping and begging. I waited all my life for my father to die and when he did I felt empty.

Voice in our head persistent. Voice in our head, barely audible. Noise comes down as a dark shade, locks out the light. The curb. Wet and black. As obstructive haze. Perseverance of unknown. Bodies in slow motion, engaged in pursuit, through action, through terse pleasure. Concentration of single acts. A hand there, the mouth doing whatever, the body's wound position. The first invitation to the trancelike state.

A black boy who lives in a corner house already looks like a man. A massive figure with truly apelike features. He embarrasses us all. Frightening to white women and children. Poor gentle ape-man-boy. Which is it then? Warriors come back to a neighborhood from war. Relief at their straight backs and scarred chests. Rueful goes out the window and we think, peace is like a shotgun aimed at the foot. If the toe is missing it's better than the whole head.

Whose becoming is this? Whose grief filled napkin? It's simply all of it. The meteoric gaps into which things get absorbed. And here the I is culling. People too disappearing into holes. Another father, one I didn't know, bought me jelly sandals for scarred feet when I was 9 or 10. We saw the Statue of Liberty and he discovered later that he locked the keys in the car. He was there that day—bones in place, heart thumping. Then gone, gone onto, suddenly, the boot trodden floor of Port Authority. Here's what is left over:

a)

b)

c) a man in a uniform

d) some relief about belonging

e) a mother's fleeting revelation

f)

g)

h)

On CNN a girl's fingers slack, empty of weapons. Behind her, shrapnel fires. My mother says, O, holy, O, O, and then presses her lips together like a snake. Our purposeful living spaces made from taciturn rooms. Entire houses of trapped utterances—mouths saturated with them. Bodies can be easily carried across borders. Tangy fissures created from single breaths. Wooden slights bribe doctors to say *This is a whole body. It's complete and useable.* We all believe that anyway. A useable body must demonstrate its use.

Near adust. Caves. Closings. Relentlessly the body leaves the bed. Does things. A day is merry and eager for prosperity. It dings dings the bell in its own head. The ritual of masking the breasts in heavy fabric, of covering the legs and feet. A face from the mirror says, I am pretty, I am pretty. Skin of opening, meant for opening. Trimmed, fastidious. Damp reasoning. Yet, adherence. Mask the breasts. Mark the skin. *You are not from here, are you?* Part tissue. *What does it feel like?* It feels like everything else. *It must be different from some other thing.* No. This is what a woman's body is. An effort in covering or not covering. A way toward exits.

Illness ensues,

not static, a doing.

A man's smoking

jacket opens. To find

a breathing that was.

Spaces that indicate collapse.

This is what punishment is.

How do we encounter the many hours past twilight? We understand that the light is something other, that it catapults us toward a desire or two if we're lucky. But lately daylight eats itself and is percussive in its chewing, a carnival of curses and thumps. Nothing is wrong. In the hours after the whinny of the long train passing, we continue to think how special we are, how born and cosmic, how just plain individual, but it is not enough. Nothing out there. Everything out there. What does it matter then, if the body climbs into a plastic car, drives into a deserted driveway and becomes another self? Elsewhere: One body found. One policeman shot. One 4-year-old girl shot. Teeter, tweeter, la, la, la, la, la. I am the I watching the I lift. Roads are short with darkness. I think, this is what they mean when they say, Savage.

0110000100100000011100000110000101111
0010011101000110100101100001011011100
0010000001101000011010010111001101111
0100011011110111001001111001001000 00
0011011110110011000100000011001 1001
1011110111001001100111011001010111 0
1000111010001101001011011100110011 1

Always the I is fissure recklessly yearning for its whole
self sense of wholeness like a potato. We walk backward
into a room because we want to restate our thoughts. All the
brown skins are glowing in this light and no one is afraid we're
all joyous but it's difficult to tell if the joy is real joy or if
it's just lack of fear. What kind of understanding will sink
into the body? It's just one body despite other previously stated
facts and when it feels something it really does. It changes, though,
and it grows up and looks completely different in the face.

I am from an undone city, a killing here, a killing there city. Safe enough. You want to hear that story. Falling people and birds. All that hanging from wires. Being adrift in place. Unweeded gardens. Trees that grow into themselves. Girls and boys locked into once slick classrooms. Yawning facades. It's really the willfulness of it all. A real sticktoitiveness. The body acts the same way it always does and has to guard against nights in parks. This is my melancholy fragrance, it tells everyone.

Pleasure documents

              socket of the

possible

              not speaking

seems like speaking

              no threat

not sought

              so many of

them since then

              if there are

origins

              how would I

know

              addiction is

like seeing stars

              wild vines

wind chest

              they say, this

is not a woman's condition

              self-made

victim

              hemmed-in

whore.

              pursuant of---

--oh, lover, I wish—

              those silver

sparkles

              strategies

and such

              for example

lovely

I realize the other women in the house think I am not a woman who belongs in the house. Or perhaps, I think there should be more women like me in the house. Filling a house with bottles of Irish whisky and stumbling through the black night to smoke. When I am here I think, all the poets have become mothers who wear flowy clothes. You can't smoke in cafes anymore anyway, so why bother. The cafes are so bright they feel like ice. Žižek whispers dirty secrets in my ear and I think of him succumbed to masturbatory habits. When I see the women in the house, I imagine them at their homes, drinking half glasses of wine and arranging flowers in kitchens. In some ways, I'm not a woman at all, but one does not have to be a woman to be here, there just aren't any men.

The lips, beleaguered and adequate anxieties—that cancer might be something you get from a room humming with digital fragrance. At 70 my mother flies on a plane for the first time and is amazed at the sensation of not moving. A sense of things that opposes the actuality of things. This is a memoir of close calls. After a set number of near misses, one catches and stops the heart. If we are delivered from evil, where do we arrive? Between the willing and the damned? This place is perceived as cuts of time, a stack of rectangles in contrasting colors. Cruelty is yellow. Accusation in blue. Perversity, a trail of microscopic scars. Pardon me if I move slowly around the edges and am fearful of ordinary lives. A system of diagnoses says, you're ok, you're not dying.

Belt pulled off the waist in fury.

It is not enough. Monstrous black fists.

Furnace boils into itself.

Bleeps of terror from hells and halls.

A twisted staircase, a twisted arm. Harms.

Harm is not enough. Is not the point

of the whole exercise. A hard, rough hand harms the

already harmed. Is harm on top of harm. Extraneous.

Cutting away. Glorious.

For today, deep light against the pungent violence of dark holds and ramp meanness. Open the case and pull out fever of meaning of meanness. Abandonment figure waits atop grassy hill. It requires a kind of discipline to wait in waiting of what one waits for. We watch from the city. It's putrid here. We just saw a man who should inspire empathy or at the very least pity. We imagine ramp and garbage. We know it says something about us. As does what we do not imagine. We know that it is our own dark hold we mention stretched toward a hill of hills, hilly and quiet as all else is quiet when howling occurs.

There is this place where the I is am now and there is the no place. Some say that it might all emanate from a place of youth as if a place of youth is the original place, but I do not believe this. That this me that might have also happened in some original place, but there must have been a me there. Or maybe I dreamed it. Maybe this is all there is.

The ripe, the gentle, the buried, the unseen, the melancholy, the yearning, the always-wanting, the always-calling, the here-I-am-please, the who-said-I-am-yours, the the the –

The pennies that hum of metal and raw
have no place here. Do not smell them.
Do not taste their rough, dirty, metallic flavor, their
hinting of some other world.
Do not place them near your mouth or fold them toward
your skin. Do not to say them,
I want to know where you've been,
the counters and pockets of your existence,
the secrets and shame that surround you.

When the bed is empty, we pull the shades to block light,

light of resemblance to remembery, long light of waiting,

an impatience in the glows of it. The here of the now and the glow

that days make in the room, without the body but with the stench

of it. So we say, *vacancy* and *abject*, against the was, against

a philosophy of once and then not. Not-being against.

A child once grew here. As lines on a wall. As

growing without knowing what would one day not be. A

gnawing grows. Grew and was. Protection is curled. Motion-

less. I envy her in her room. Hers with paint and dolls and hand-

prints. Great green and glowing under blankets with a hand

that nurtures the heart of the mouth, purrs into mouth, loves

the heart. Heart beating within another—blushing blood—

God, the beating, lit, and doing what it does.

I am a murderer. All these fissures undoing me all the time. All these reminiscences. In the gleaming super super store, I stock the cart with a cable wire, duct tape, a 64-pack of Scott extra soft toilet paper. And simultaneously, a [quaked] darkness. Some dragging him from the crime scene to the burial place. The house has room after room after room. The hill is quiet. No one will ever find him.

Every night the body winds through the unlit corridors of the house. It tries to be quiet but there is nothing more quiet than the quiet itself. At the first glimpse of sun rising, panic. We are separated from the city. If this is a room in the country then there are other rooms like this one. A boy smells of hemp and bug spray. Cool cats, you know, float up, a mystery. Domesticity lingers.

> *Women in dresses, men in shirts.*
> *Just an approach—*
> *—a waiting or*
> *since there is time, some tea*
> > *and wallpaper.*

The body-carts are of a particular shape and size so everyone doesn't have one. We are assured that there were errors. Sleep, little bodies, sleep.

Almost every dirt road leads to some dirt hole. One might have to pass a 15-room house, but there will be a dirt hole. There always is. Hole is a terrible word. If a child says, I put my finger down a hole, it sounds dirty. Dirty dirt hole. This is the first clue: avoid holes. If you can't, lie about it. Know what numbers know: their belonging. My parents' house in Connecticut is 314. My house now is 275. Three numbers are good. Three of anything is good. If there is a goodness in numbers, then there is a puzzle. Myopic vision alters the thing in front of the eyes. If holes are bad, then what am I? Are holes things with ends to them, or do they go on forever? One must decide. An aching toward a hole is an aching toward an invisibility. This is why it's difficult to be a girl. But, it's harder, much harder, to be the hole filler, the one who pushes up into an indefinable place, what's at the end of the road, and for sure, likened to something it is not, because no one knows what it is and there you are trying so desperately to do what you are supposed to do. I, too, am sick with worry. A shovel is in the hand. A cuff has bound the wrist. One thing is filled, another excavated. That's the trick. There is nothing in the world that is not exactly like this.

So so swift, sift of flour for baking. So so soft. As butter. As wind. This is the frame of the seeing, of recollection, what the child has hung her hat on. The hands and the mother's hands and baking. When they were sincere. When they mapped love in a cake. Tell me, what is toothy about this? Why does it matter? Lonely is lost in this. Lonely is my mother in a chair with mail order catalogs and small dinners. A patient man once asked, Are you a friend? I said, I am a friend, if you are not a fiend. So so watermelon red. So so like the ambivalence of soldiers. Our hands reach into a jar for cookies. We are here in this pungent room. The I of the I is absolutely, is promisingly approaching a, or, the way back.

Falls and lifts at same time pulls up and sideways
and unsure. Winter. I'm drifting. Hoods and cloaks
gather as in, *Here We Are*, bright heart lifts too. Sweet-
hearts before knew me as I was then, as the world was
then, not, it always seems as broken but unpredictable
as snow as a weapon. *She's a slick one*, they'd say, or
Hey there lucky, perfect belligerence   a little push.

Wuuh swept up   chest cavern   bloating as inverse
so we say deserted or what was here   Wuuh like fire.
Heave tubes a body makes those   gesture of up traces silver.
Could not see-saw worry hard about sand pit and ankles
hands on white metal. Kids jump off and make the way go
down and say ahhhhhhhh. These are regular things. We eat.
We enjoy the food spaghetti   sandwiches and hot cross rolls butter
secret spills out. I'm a hero today because everything is outside
of this body really strong and catapulting a bunch of people
into the room and outside themselves too.

A man enters a hospital. They brush him off and prop him up, his dark-eyed haunt hidden among wires and plugs. A medical text might fixate on what's working in the body and what's not working in order to determine who is alive and who is dead. We know better. Somewhere along the way I fell into the deep end of the pool. Swimming eludes me. Then clunk until flesh and lungs lie in wait. Where is there? I want to ask him, What is lacking? The facts of the incident are forgotten many times. Body. Neighbor. Yard. Psych ward. Forgetting is a way of misremembering the present. If a father once loved a son, then this is a son who was once loved by the father. I am breathless in the heat and imagine, *It is finished, you know?* In finishing, one forgets.

However, the Williamsburg Bridge, its tenacious being and,

However, that I walked before it, could have been me, of course,

Rousing the specificity of things that happen in darkness, or

However cathedrals were made with seats for holiness as if the body

Could be contained—these are the dirtiest bodies, mackerel and other fish—

Could be latched up, un-regarded, un-tenacious,

Where the dancers might go to die. And, however humble or saying,

Christ, forgive me, there it is the Williamsburg Bridge, slim as learning,

A terminal medication, and the words, *try try,* and, *honey, I'm listening, I swear,*

However, the bridge, the forgotten bridge, mushrooming in revision,

A real stinker in relation to its prescient cousins, the unknowing, the dumb.

Coda

No one speaks of him, the dead, irrevocably unnamed. Thought of once in certain ways. B-force. Magnitudes of what happens when. Words only when. An 8-track tape played Billy Eckstine singing, *If I caused you pain, I know I'm to blame.* Once. The withered, worn body prostrate and dry in a twin bed. It is white with ash. White as the walls will become later. What was once a room to die in.

The blood, we were told, will interrogate the bones, will cut microscopic holes. If there are bones more fragile than these, we do not know them. Larger than the organs in the body, any seer can see what wasting is.

In lieu of a stained coffee cup or an unframed photo taped to a mirror. They come. *Tell us your empty story,* they say. Remember the bullet hole on your thigh, emblem from another world? Remember the Army planes that clunked toward some distance? There must have been other black boys leaving the chattering open fields of bent over bodies. Others who. Then those who could not. And did. But did not know until.

Others with him. In a mire of killing. They hunker down to avoid being noticed. If they are not noticed, then maybe they will live. If they do survive, what will survival be? If they are not noticed, will being unnoticed be a way to live?

Everyday something different occurs. One day, there are fronds, a farm, and a whorehouse. In the whorehouse, boys do what men might do. Slate gift in the hearts of boys. In the whorehouse the boys are not afraid. They are men. Are the girls women? Or are the girls another story? Outside the whorehouse, this boy, once a man, now dead, becomes precise. A sharp edge against the sun.

Acknowledgements

Many grateful thanks to the magazines and anthologies in which versions of poems first appeared: *Daedalus: A Journal of the American Arts & Sciences, Encyclopedia Project* F-K, *Hambone, Jubilat, La Fovea, Tuesday Journal: An Art Project,* and *Writing Self and Community: African-American Poetry After the Civil Rights Movement.*

Thanks, too, to the many reading series, conferences, and other venues that provided opportunities for me to read from this work: &Now: A Conference on Innovative Writing and the Literary Arts, Antioch University, Baltimore Public Library, Callaloo Mini Conference: *Literature, Culture, & Critique,* David Buuck's reading series, Duquesne University's *Lifting Belly High: Women's Poetry Since 1900,* Minor American Reading Series, Penn State University Altoona, Penn State University State College, The Pittsburgh Cultural Trust, The Poetry Project at St. Marks, The Poetry Society of America & The Boston College Howard Gotlieb Archival Research Center's *State of the Art: African-American Poetry Today,* Post_Moot Poetry and Performance Convocation, Reading Series Between A and B, Small Press Traffic, Segue at Bowery Poetry Club, and the SUNY Buffalo Poetics Program.

This book would not exist without my wonderful writing communities—the mind-blowingly creative people who inspire me everyday: the Black Took Collective (Duriel E. Harris and Ronaldo Wilson) and the Southampton Writers Project (Nicole Hefner Callihan, Kristin Dombek, Stephanie K. Hopkins, and Marion Wrenn).

Deep gratitude to the institutions that supported this work when it was in process: Cave Canem Foundation, the American Academy of Arts and Sciences, and Ragdale Foundation.

I am forever indebted to you all.

Special thanks to Fanny Howe for selecting this collection.

Dawn Lundy Martin

Dawn Lundy Martin is also the author of *A Gathering of Matter/A Matter of Gathering* (2007) and *The Morning Hour* (2003). She is co-founder of the Black Took Collective, a group of experimental black poets; one of four founders of the Third Wave Founda-tion in New York, a femi-nist, activist foundation that works nationally to support young women and transgen-

der youth ages 15 to 30; and co-editor of a collection of essays, *The Fire This Time: Young Activists and The New Feminism* (2004). An assistant professor of English at the University of Pittsburgh, Martin lives in Pittsburgh and Westhampton, New York.

ISBN: 978-0-9844598-4-1

Design and typesetting by HR Hegnauer
Cover art: detail from "(THEM) TREES ...(THEM) CHANGES"
by Arnold J. Kemp, 2009
Courtesy of the artist
Text set in Meridian

Cataloging-in-publication data is available
From the Library of Congress

Distributed by University Press of New England
One Court Street
Lebanon, NH 03766
www.upne.com

Nightboat Books
Callicoon, New York
www.nightboat.org

Nightboat Books

Nightboat Books, a nonprofit organization, seeks to develop audiences for writers whose work resists convention and transcends boundaries. We publish books rich with poignancy, intelligence, and risk. Please visit our website, www.nightboat.org, to learn about our titles and how you can support our future publications.

The following individuals have supported the publication of this book. We thank them for their generosity and commitment to the mission of Nightboat Books:

Kazim Ali
Jennifer Chapis
Sarah Heller
Elizabeth Motika
Laura Sejen
Benjamin Taylor

This book has been made possible, in part, by a grant from the New York State Council on the Arts Literature Program.

State of the Arts

NYSCA